WORLD OF WOW WONDER

THE AWESOME BOOK OF

THE UNIVERSE

Get ready to hear your kids say, "Wow! That's awesome!" as they dive into this fun, informative, question-answering series of books! Students—and teachers and parents—will learn things about the world around them that they never knew before!

This approach to education seeks to promote an interest in learning by answering questions kids have always wondered about. When books answer questions that kids already want to know the answers to, kids love to read those books, fostering a love for reading and learning, the true keys to lifelong education.

Colorful graphics are labeled and explained to connect with visual learners, while entertaining explanations of each subject will connect with those who prefer reading or listening as their learning style.

This educational series makes learning fun through many levels of interaction. The in-depth information combined with fantastic illustrations promote learning and retention, while question and answer boxes reinforce the subject matter to promote higher order thinking.

Teachers and parents love this series because it engages young people, sparking an interest and desire in learning. It doesn't feel like work to learn about a new subject with books this interactive and interesting.

This set of books will be an addition to your home or classroom library that everyone will enjoy. And, before you know it, you too will be saying, "Wow! That's awesome!"

"People cannot learn by having information pressed into their brains. Knowledge has to be sucked into the brain, not pushed in. First, one must create a state of mind that craves knowledge, interest, and wonder. You can teach only by creating an urge to know." - Victor Weisskopf

© 2014 Flowerpot Press

Contents under license
from Aladdin Books Ltd.

Flowerpot Press
142 2nd Avenue North
Franklin, TN 37064

Flowerpot Press is a
division of Kamalu LLC,
Franklin, TN, U.S.A. and
Flowerpot Children's Press,
Inc.,Oakville, ON, Canada.

ISBN 978-1-77093-809-0

Illustrators:
Ian Thompson
Graham White
Simon Tegg
Cartoons: Jo Moore

American Edition Editor:
Johannah Gilman Paiva

Designer:
Simon Morse

American Redesign:
Jonas Fearon Bell

Printed in China.

CONTENTS

INTRODUCTION

When you look up into the dark sky at night, have you ever wondered what is out there? You may know that the Earth is part of the solar system, but what is beyond that?

This book will take you off into the far reaches of the universe. Find out how new planets are formed, discover how gravity works, and learn about the Big Bang that started it all, and the Big Crunch that may end it all.

• In this book, a billion is one thousand million.

On-the-spot quiz!

Q: Why watch out for these boxes?

A: They give answers to the space questions you always wanted to ask.

Zoom in on...

Space Bits

Look out for these boxes to take a closer look at space features.

Awesome Facts

Watch out for these diamonds to learn more about the truly weird and wonderful facts about space and the universe in which we live.

THE UNIVERSE

The universe is very, very, very big—bigger than anything you can possibly imagine. It is not just all the stars, planets, and galaxies, but all the empty space in between. In fact, the universe is everything that exists, from the tiniest bit of an atom to entire galaxies.

Which planet is named after the Roman goddess of love?

Pluto

Uranus

Saturn

Neptune

Jupiter

Mars

Earth

Venus

Sun

Mercury

Q: How big is our solar system?

A: Our solar system is so large, it would take you over 5,000 years driving in a fast car to get to Pluto, one of the five minor planets in our solar system.

No one knows just how big the universe is, or even whether it has a definite edge. Some astronomers think it goes on forever. Others believe it is shaped like a doughnut. But with powerful telescopes scientists can see incredibly bright objects called "quasars," which they believe may be on the edge of the universe. These could be as far as 7.45 billion trillion miles (12 billion trillion kilometers) away.

Awesome Facts
Our galaxy, the Milky Way, seems huge, but the universe contains at least 100 billion galaxies like ours.

THE BIG BANG

Scientists hypothesize that the universe began with an enormous explosion. One moment there was nothing, the next, there was a tiny, unbelievably hot, dense ball, containing all the matter in the universe today. Then a moment later, the universe existed, blasting itself into life with the biggest explosion of all time—the Big Bang.

2

1

? **Q: How do we know about the Big Bang?**

A: Every galaxy in the universe is zooming away from ours. This shows the universe is expanding. By plotting back from the past how it has expanded, astronomers have worked out that the universe began about 13 billion years ago.

1. No one knows quite why it all started, but scientists think it all began with a small, incredibly hot ball. In the first split second, this grew to the size of a football, and then cooled down rapidly.

2. Gravity behaved very strangely. Instead of pulling things together, it blew them apart, and the universe expanded at terrific speed. In a split second, it grew bigger than a galaxy.

3

3. As the universe expanded, it cooled, and tiny particles of energy and matter began to appear. These particles formed a dense, immensely thick soup.

4. After about 3 minutes, gravity began to behave as it does now, drawing things together. Particles joined to make atoms, atoms joined to make gases, such as hydrogen and helium.

4

5. Gases clumped into clouds. After several hundred million years, these clouds began to form stars and galaxies. These galaxies merged into clusters and superclusters, and much later the Sun and solar system were formed. The universe is still expanding and new planets and stars are still being formed.

5

GRAVITY

Every bit of matter in the universe is pulled towards every other bit by an invisible force called "gravity." It is what keeps you on the ground and holds the solar system and the whole universe together.

Jupiter is huge and is, in some ways, more like a star than a planet. Made mostly of hydrogen and helium, like the Sun, its strong gravity squeezes these gases until they are hot.

Earth's gravity pulls things to the ground—unless, like rockets, they use powerful engines to push in the opposite direction. Gravity also pulls the Moon into orbit around the Earth.

Exploring rocket

Satellite rocket

Jet

The Sun's gravity keeps Earth in orbit around it.

Sun

Moon's orbit

Satellite's orbit

Earth's orbit

Gravity is a mutual attraction between every bit of matter. A skydiver has a gravity that pulls, and he falls because his and the Earth pull each other together. But he falls to the Earth rather than Earth falling to him because the Earth is much heavier and pulls so strongly.

Q: How is gravity used to guess the size of stars?

A: The pull of gravity between two things like planets or stars depends on how massive they are, and how far apart they are. Astronomers can often tell how big a star is from how strongly its gravity appears to pull on nearby stars or planets.

STARS

Stars are the basic units of the universe. There are eight planets in our solar system that orbit our star, the Sun. However, astronomers have found at least 50 other planets in the universe that circle other stars.

Awesome Facts

There is a planet circling the distant star 51 Pegasi. Temperatures there are probably a scorching 2,372°F (1,300 °C), and a year lasts just 4 days.

① 1

Zoom in on...

New Worlds

Even when they cannot see a new planet directly, astronomers may see a disc of matter around a star in which new planets are forming.

Distant stars may have planets circling them, which are too small to see, even with a powerful telescope. But as a planet circles a star, its gravity pulls the star slightly to and from. Astronomers notice that the star's light turns a little redder when the planet is pulling the star away from the Earth. It turns bluer when the planet pulls the star towards Earth.

Astronomers think planets form from vast discs of gas and dust that spin around certain stars (1). Gravity makes the discs clump together in places to form new planets (2).

THE GROWING UNIVERSE

The universe is incredibly big, and it is getting bigger! We know this because every star we can see is rushing away from us. The further away a star is, the faster it is whizzing away.

Awesome Facts
The nearest star, Alpha Centauri, is 4.2 light-years away from Earth. This means light would take 4.2 years to travel from this star to Earth.

Astronomers can tell from a star's color how fast it is moving. As it zooms away, the light waves get stretched out behind it. Stretched light waves look redder. The faster it is moving, the more the waves are stretched, and the redder it looks.

To see why galaxies move further apart as the universe expands, try this with a balloon: stick paper stars on a partly inflated balloon to represent the galaxies. Then, blow up the balloon more. You can see the stars (galaxies) moving further apart as the balloon gets bigger.

LIGHT AND RADIATION

All the time, every second of the day and night, the stars are beaming energy called "radiation" at us here on Earth. Some of this radiation, called "visible light," is the light we can see. Most radiation, though, is invisible, coming in waves that our eyes cannot detect.

Our eyes can see only visible light. But astronomers have built special telescopes that pick up invisible radiation, such as X-rays and radio waves. This means we can see much more of the stars and galaxies than our eyes alone show us. Indeed, there are stars such as Scorpius X-1 and Cygnus X-1 that are known mostly by their X-ray and radio signals.

How Light Travels

We know that light and other kinds of radiation travel in a straight line, faster than anything else in the universe. But scientists were long unsure whether light moved like waves in the sea, or like a bouncing ball. They now believe it is a combination of both—minute packets of vibrating energy called "photons."

Awesome Facts

Astronomers' telescopes can register light sent out by distant stars billions of years ago. This light can help us discover the history of the universe.

STAR CLUSTERS

Stars are not spread evenly across space. Instead, they huddle together in clumps called "clusters," attracted by their own mutual gravity. New clusters are forming all the time, but some are billions of years old.

With the Hubble Space Telescope, astronomers found that clusters contain more stars than were visible before. Hubble showed that this cluster, NGC 1850 (right), thought to contain only about 1,000 stars, actually contains at least 10,000 stars.

What is the other name for the Pleiades?

Pleiades

The newest clusters are called "open clusters" and contain several hundred stars. The Pleiades open cluster in the constellation of Taurus is one of the few clusters in which some individual stars can be seen with the naked eye. However, it also contains hundreds too faint for you to see.

Globular clusters

Around the edge of galaxies there are about 140 large, old clusters called "globular clusters" (left). There are often 100,000 stars in a globular cluster, and sometimes up to a million. As the galaxy spins around, so do these clusters, taking about 100 million years to go around the galaxy once.

Elliptical

Barred spiral

GALAXIES

Just as stars are gathered in clusters, so clusters of stars are clumped into vast star cities called "galaxies." The biggest galaxies are incredibly large and can contain thousands of billions of stars.

Galaxies zoom around in all directions. Every now and then they crash into each other. Irregular galaxies, like the Small Magellanic Cloud, may be the debris from such a galactic pile-up.

?

Q: How old are galaxies?

A: Scientists cannot agree how old galaxies are. Most believe that many elliptical galaxies date back almost to the dawn of time and are at least ten billion years old!

Most galaxies are spiral in shape. A quarter of all galaxies are irregular. Some galaxies are barred spirals. The galaxies are round or fried-egg-shaped elliptical galaxies.

Irregular

The Andromeda galaxy is the nearest to the Milky Way. It is still so far away that without a telescope it looks just like a faint blur. Two million light-years away, it is the furthest thing we can see with the naked eye.

Spiral

THE MILKY WAY

Our Sun is just one of the 100 billion stars grouped together in a galaxy called "the Milky Way." The Milky Way is often called "the Galaxy," but is actually just one of more than 30 billion spiral galaxies in the universe.

Canis Major

Puppis

Vela

Centaurus

Crux

Muca

Carina

Spot the group of stars represented by a dog.

Triangulum Australe

Ara

Our Sun, with its solar system of planets, is just one of millions of stars on one of the arms of the Milky Way. The whole galaxy sweeps the Sun around at nearly 62 million miles per hour (100 million kilometers per hour)! The sun goes around the galaxy once in just 225 million years.

Gemini

Cassiopeia

Perseus

Monoceros

The Milky Way contains some of the night sky's most brilliant groups of stars, some of which are labeled here, but this is just a tiny fraction of the galaxy as a whole.

Orion

 Q: Why is it called the Milky Way?

A: If you're far from town on a dark, clear night, you can see a hazy band of light stretching across the sky. You are actually seeing an edge-on view of the Milky Way galaxy with its countless stars. People long ago called it the Milky Way because it looked like someone had spilled milk across the sky.

BLACK HOLES

Black holes are points in space where gravity is so strong that it sucks in everything. These points even suck in light so they can't be seen. This is why they are called "black" holes.

Awesome Facts
If you fell into a black hole, you would be stretched out thinner than spaghetti by its unimaginably powerful gravity.

Some black holes probably form when a huge star burns out. It is squeezed so tightly by its own gravity that all of its matter is crushed into a tiny point before it vanishes completely.

Some scientists think there are white holes, too. If black holes are like plugholes sucking in everything, then white holes are fountains, where it all gushes out. If we could join a black hole to a white hole, perhaps we could create a tunnel, or a shortcut, through space.

Black hole

White hole

Black hole and white hole join, forming a tunnel.

No one has spotted a black hole for sure, but astronomers are fairly confident there are black holes linked to at least seven double stars. The most likely candidate for a black hole is the double star V404 Cygni.

Enormous black holes may be at the heart of every galaxy, including the Milky Way. These black holes may contain as much matter as millions of suns, in a space no bigger than the solar system.

This picture shows a black hole as a funnel, because matter, radiation, and even space and time, are sucked into a black hole like water down a drain. In fact, a black hole is small and round, and its surface is called an "event horizon." If you go beyond the event horizon, you go out of space and time into nothingness.

ACTIVE GALAXIES

We see many galaxies because they beam out visible light, but there are some that beam out powerful surges of X-rays, radio waves, and other invisible forms of radiation. Astronomers call these galaxies "active galaxies."

When astronomers look at the galaxy Centaurus-A using X-rays, they see a band of bright spots on either side of the galaxy's core. They believe these bright spots are gas particles, shot out of the core of a black hole, surging through the galaxy's magnetic field.

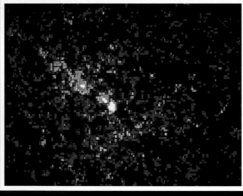

The jets sent out by the black hole at the core of the Centaurus-A galaxy generate X-rays and radio waves. They beam out radio signals that make the most powerful radio beacon on Earth seem very weak by comparison. The gas jets are 100 times larger than our entire galaxy.

An active galaxy beams out awesome amounts of energy. Astronomers think the source of all this power is a massive black hole that sucks in entire stars. As the black hole shreds a star, it spews out jets of gas, which generate X-rays and radio waves.

A photo of the galaxy Centaurus-A (above) shows a different view from the X-ray photo (left). The galaxy's core is believed to be a massive disc of gas spinning around a huge black hole.

SUPERSTRUCTURES

Just as clusters of stars form galaxies, so galaxies group to form even larger structures. Our Milky Way galaxy is over 100,000 light-years across, but it is just part of a group of 40 galaxies called the "Local Group."

Local Group

Milky Way

Just as galaxies form the Local Group, so the Local Group is clumped with other groups of galaxies to form clusters of thousands of galaxies. Half a dozen or so clusters are, in turn, grouped into large superclusters 200 million light-years across.

Cluster of galaxies

Superclusters

Superclusters are grouped in loops and superwalls, separated by voids 400 million light-years across.

Zoom in on...

Great Wall

The biggest known structure in the universe is the Great Wall. It is a superwall, a group of superclusters, some 500 million light-years long, but even this may not be the biggest structure; there may even be structures three billion light-years across!

THE BIG CRUNCH

Scientists are looking into the sky for clues about the fate of the universe. Will it go on growing forever—the open universe? Will it stop growing and just stay the same size—steady state? Or will it eventually shrink again—the Big Crunch?

Q: What is the Big Crunch?

A: If there is a lot of invisible matter in the universe, its gravity will pull the universe back together again. The universe will start to shrink, until it all ends up the size of a marble: the Big Crunch.

Current theories suggest our universe may be just one of many in existence. Lots of universes may be bubbling up all the time beyond space and time.

1. Continual expansion

2. Universe remains steady

3. Big Crunch

The fate of the universe probably depends on how much invisible matter there is to hold it together. If there is too little, the universe will go on getting gradually bigger (1), if there is more, it will remain steady (2), if there is more still, it will all end in the Big Crunch (3).

UNIVERSE FACTS

The universe is enormous and it can be difficult to understand its size. Below is a chart that will give you some idea of the proportions of the universe!

Milky Way
100,000 light-years
across

Andromeda
Our nearest galaxy, 2 million
light-years from Earth

Our solar system
13 light-hours across

Alpha Centauri
Our nearest star
system, 4.2 light-years
from Earth

Pluto
Minor planet,
5.5
light-hours
from Earth

Earth

Moon
1 light-second
from Earth

Sun
Our star, 8
light-minutes
from Earth

GLOSSARY

Active galaxy
A galaxy that emits huge amounts of radiation, including radio waves and X-rays. Astronomers believe that active galaxies have a black hole at their center.

Big Bang
A huge explosion about 13 billion years ago that many astronomers believe started the universe.

Big Crunch
A possible end to the universe. This could occur if all the matter in the universe is pulled together by gravity, ending in a Big Crunch.

Black hole
The remains of a huge star that has exploded and collapsed in on itself. The gravity is so strong that not even light can escape.

Constellations
A group of stars in the night sky. Astronomers recognize 88 of them.

Galaxy
An enormous cluster of stars. Each galaxy can contain many billions of stars. Galaxies can be spiral, barred spiral, elliptical, or irregular. Our galaxy is the Milky Way.

Gravity
A force that attracts every object in the universe to every other object. The solar system is held together mainly by the Sun's gravitational pull.

Light-year
A unit used to measure distance in space. It is the distance light travels in one year: about 6 million miles (9.6 million kilometers).

Matter
Any material that exists and takes up space.

Photon
A tiny packet of vibrating energy.

Quasar
An object in space that emits an enormous amount of energy. Quasars are thought to be at the center of very distant galaxies.

Radiation
Energy that can be visible light, or waves that our eyes cannot see, such as X-rays or radio waves.

Solar system
The group of major planets, including Earth, and minor planets that orbit the Sun.

Universe
Everything that exists, from the tiniest atoms to entire galaxies, and beyond.

Void
An empty space or area.

INDEX

Picture credits
Abbreviations: t-top, m-middle, b-bottom, r-right, l-left
1bl, 16 – STScl/Galaxy Picture Library. 1br, 14, 17tr – Ross Ressmeyer/CORBIS. 9 – Alistair Wright; The Military Picture Library/CORBIS. 10 – NASA. 14br – NASA. 17ml, 25 – CORBIS. 19tr – Michael Stecker/Galaxy Picture Library. 24 – Dr. Eric Feigelson/Science Photo Library.